Everybody Has Feelings
Todos Tenemos Sentimientos

The Moods of Children
as photographed by **Charles E. Avery**

gryphon house
Beltsville, Maryland

Translation:
Sandra Marulanda
•
Book and cover design:
Deb Figen
ART & DESIGN SEVICES

Published and Distributed by Gryphon House, Inc.
10726 Tucker Street, Beltsville Maryland 20705
Toll free orders (800) 638-0928 or Fax: (301) 595-0051

Library of Congress Cataloging-in-Publication Data
Avery, Charles E., 1938-
    Everybody has feelings = Todos tenemos sentimientos : the moods of children / as photographed by Charles E. Avery : [translation, Sandra Marulanda].
    P.   cm.
    Originally published: Seattle, Wash. : Open Hand Pub. : New York.
NY : Distributed by Talman Co., cl992.
    Summary: Photographs of children and text in both English and Spanish explore a wide range of human emotions.
    ISBN 0-87659-197-7
    1. Emotions--Juvenile literature.   [1. Emotions.   2. Spanish language materials--Bilingual.]   I. Title.   II. Title: Todos tenemos sentimientos.
    [BF561.A84 1998]
    152.4'022'2--DC21   97-47454
                                                                          CIP
                                                                          AC

Originally published by Open Hand Publishers

In Spanish, the endings of many adjectives indicate gender. Where there are both male and female children in the same photo or section, the gender of the adjective corresponds to the majority of the people pictured.

En español las terminaciones de muchos adjetivos indican el género. Donde hay niños y niñas en una misma foto o seccíon, el género del adjetivo corresponderá a la mayoría.

Printed in Korea

Dedication

To all the brave children of the planet...

I wish you peace, health, happiness and good fortune.

•

A todos los niños valientes del planeta...

les deseo paz, salud, felicidad y dicha.

Sometimes
I feel happy

•

A veces
me siento feliz

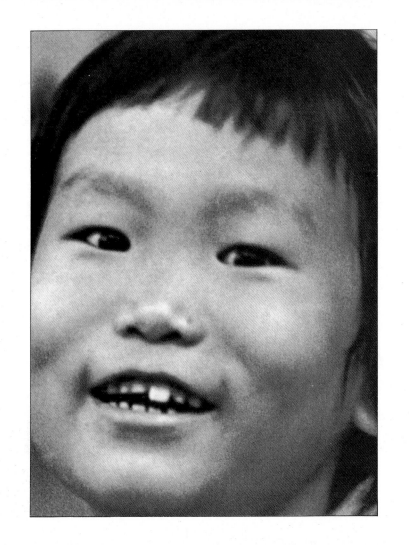

sad

•

triste

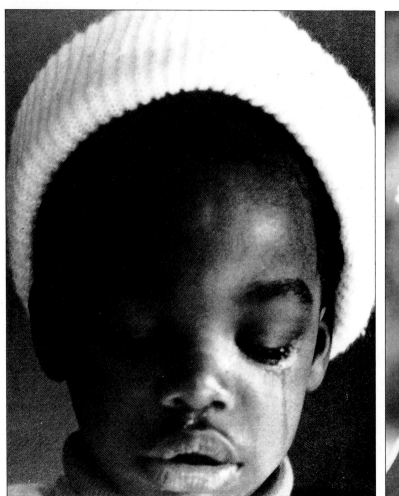

lonely

•

solo

Sometimes
I like to be alone

•

A veces
me gusta estar solo

Sometimes
I feel friendly

●

A veces
me siento amigable

curious

•

curioso

talkative

●

hablador

playful • juguetón

excited

•

animado

Sometimes
I feel proud

•

A veces
me siento
orgulloso

strong • fuerte

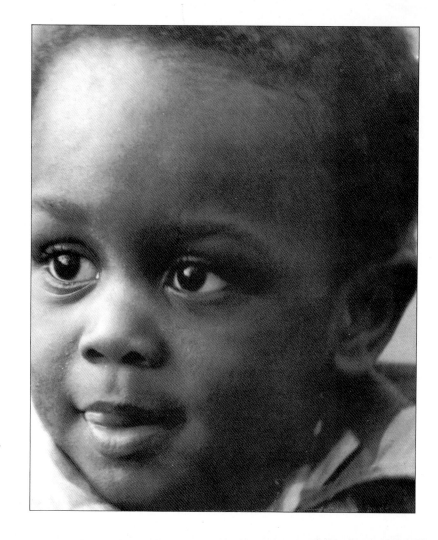

hungry • hambrienta

angry • furioso

Sometimes
I have mixed
feelings
•
A veces
tengo una
mezcla de
sentimientos

Sometimes I feel shy

•

A veces me siento tímida

safe and trusting

•

seguro y confiado

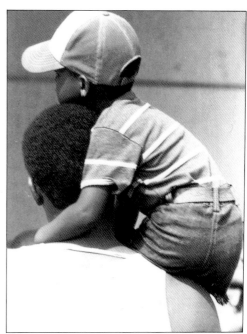

Sometimes I feel love

●

A veces me siento amada

CHARLES AVERY was born in Atlanta, Georgia. He grew up in Harlem and attended New York public schools, then studied at the School of Visual Arts. He served for two years in the armed forces.

Mr. Avery is the author of *Black Traces,* a collection of photographs and poems which express the dignity and strength of Black Americans. He lives in North Plainfield, New Jersey. He works as a free-lance photographer and as a senior assistant librarian.